How to use this book

This book is divided into three parts. The cover and centre colour pages form the arena. The black and white pages of gladiators and animals are for you to pull out, colour in and cut out. The other colour pages, including this one, are full of arena facts and how a gladiator lived, trained and fought. Don't pull these pages out. There is a glossary on the inside back cover to explain tricky words.

Open the cover into a triangle. Fold the smaller flap over the book and push the arena tabs into the slots. Place on a flat surface.

Colour the pictures before cutting them out. Keep them in an envelope tucked into the book.

Attach the two flaps to the sides and slot in the third piece to form the arena.

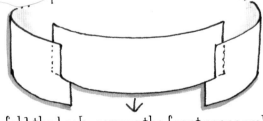

To fold the book, remove the front arena wall and fold in the other two flaps.

Templates

Tape a piece of tracing paper over the template or image. Trace in pencil.

Turn the tracing paper over and scribble over the lines with a pencil.

Turn over again and tape on to card or paper. Re-trace firmly over the lines. Remove the tracing paper.

What is an arena?

An arena is the central part of an amphitheatre where the action took place. It was covered in sand to soak up the blood from the fights! Nearly every city in the Roman Empire had an arena but the Colosseum in Rome was the grandest of all.

   The Colosseum could seat 50,000 people. It had 80 entrances and was designed so cleverly that it could be emptied in minutes in case of fire. Everyone came, with the poorest sitting at the top and the rich seated near the arena.

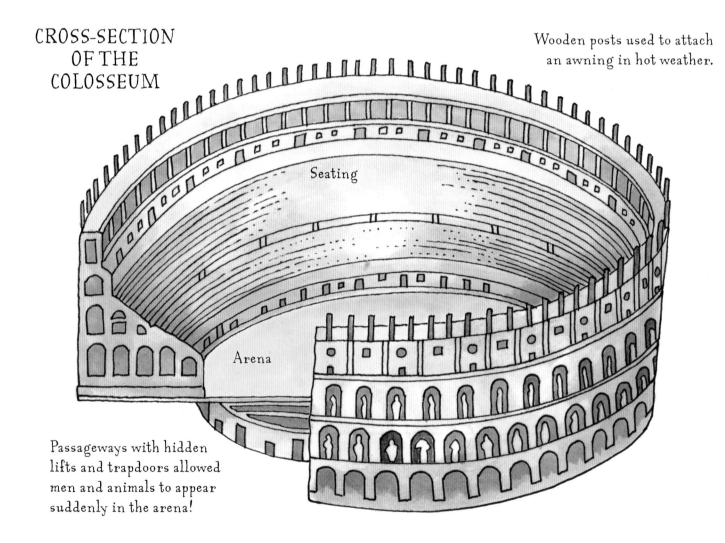

CROSS-SECTION OF THE COLOSSEUM

Wooden posts used to attach an awning in hot weather.

Seating

Arena

Passageways with hidden lifts and trapdoors allowed men and animals to appear suddenly in the arena!

The 'games' were put on by wealthy politicians and Emperors to show off their power and to keep the people happy. The day would include fights with wild animals and executions of criminals and Christians. In the afternoon, the highlight would be the gladiatorial fights. These fights and deaths were seen as normal entertainment – a bit like watching the television today!

What is a gladiator?

Gladiators were men (and very occasionally women) trained to fight to entertain people. Most were slaves and criminals but sometimes a free-born man would also take the gladiatorial oath, 'I will endure to be burned, to be bound, to be beaten and to be killed by the sword.'

Bronze helmet worn by one of the more heavily armed gladiators.

Small bronze statuettes of gladiators

Most gladiators died young but some did live to buy their freedom.

Gladiators fought in pairs or groups. Bets were taken and the arena would buzz with excitement.

A fallen gladiator about to be killed could appeal to the Emperor for mercy. He would look to the crowd who would give a 'thumbs up' for a reprieve and 'thumbs down' for a killing.

Gladiators lived in guarded barracks. They were taught to fight, using wooden weapons, by a LANISTA (trainer). They were fed a high-energy diet and given the best medical treatment. This all cost a lot and when a gladiator was killed the person putting on the games had to pay the owner.

Fighting to the death

There were several types of gladiators, each using different weapons, armour and styles of fighting. Some wore heavy armour which meant they were better protected but slower moving. Others wore very little armour so that they were more vulnerable but could move more quickly.

SAMNITE
Greave on left leg. Helmet with a visor and a plume. Large rectangular shield and armed with a sword.

RETARIUS
Loin cloth, no armour. Metal protector on left arm and shoulder. Armed with dagger and trident. Carried a net in which to capture his opponent.

Colour the pictures, then cut them out.
Bend along the dotted lines
and stand them up.

RETARIUS

SAMNITE

THRACIAN

GLADIATORS FIGHTING

GLADIATORS FIGHTING

Place gladiators in
the arena to fight.

ASKING FOR MERCY

DRAGGING THE DEAD AWAY

VICTORIOUS GLADIATOR

LANISTA
(trainer)

OPENING PARADE

PEOPLE GOING TO THE GAMES

Stand the arena on a flat surface. Place the figures, animals and other cut-outs in and around it.

PAINTED ADVERTISEMENTS FOR GAMES

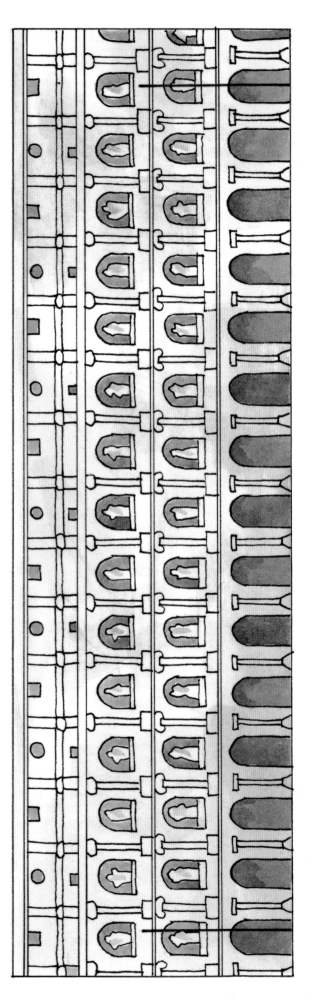

Slot this piece on to both ends of the two flaps, forming the oval arena.

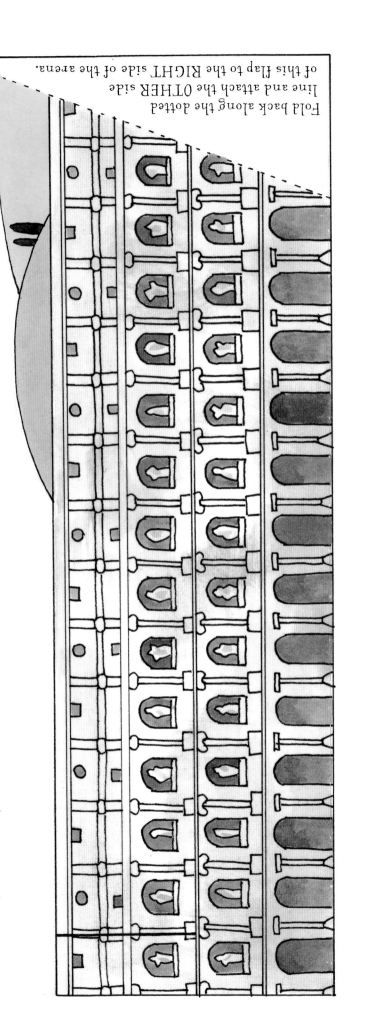

Fold back along the dotted
line and attach the OTHER side
of this flap to the RIGHT side of the arena.

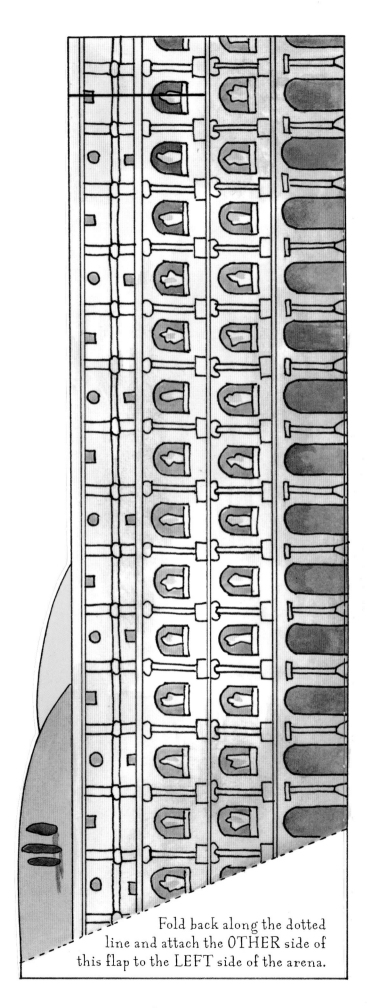

Fold back along the dotted
line and attach the OTHER side of
this flap to the LEFT side of the arena.

LION

POUNCING TIGER

BEAR

STAMPEDING ELEPHANT

FIGHTING A LEOPARD

HUNTING DEER

CHARIOTEER

Colour the teams in one of the Roman stables' colours – blue, red, white or green. Mark out an oval and have a race. Seven laps!

CHARIOTEER

The names and appearances of the gladiators were based on Barbarians. These were people who were seen as enemies of Rome and who had been conquered. The gladiators usually fought in pairs, one of each type. They fought to the death.

THRACIAN

Greaves on both legs, protector on left arm. Helmet with wide brim. Small square shield and armed with a curved short dagger.

Make a mosaic

Mosaics are pictures made with small pieces of coloured stone and glass. The Romans decorated the walls and floors of buildings with these. Much of what we know today about gladiators and the spectacles held in Roman arenas comes from mosaics found in excavated villas. Here's how to make your own mosaic using coloured paper.

Old magazines or coloured papers
23-cm square piece of paper
Tracing paper, pencil and black felt-tip
Scissors and glue

Choose a gladiator from the centre spread. Follow the instructions on the first page to trace him on to the centre of the square paper.

Cut pieces of coloured magazine pages or paper into tiny squares. Odd corners will be filled with pieces cut to fit.

Start gluing the pieces in position inside the gladiator, leaving tiny gaps in between. Fill in all one colour at a time. When the gladiator is finished, draw in details with the pen.

Now fill in the background. Begin next to the gladiator and continue until 2 cm away from the paper's edge. Add a pattern to make a border that frames your mosaic.

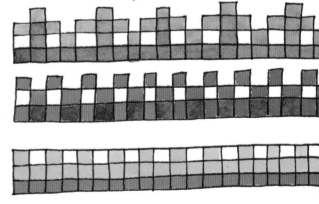

Write gladiator name.

Chariot racing

Many Roman cities also had a circus or stadium as well as an amphitheatre. This was where chariot races were held. The largest, CIRCUS MAXIMUS in Rome, held a quarter of a million people!

Small chariots were pulled by two or four horses. The driver stood in the chariot. The race lasted for seven laps of the track. It was very dangerous, especially on the tight bends, and took great skill and daring.

The drivers wore different colours, depending on the stable they raced for. People would follow them, bet on them and even fight other fans. It was like supporting a favourite football team.

The drivers, or charioteers, only wore a light helmet for protection. The reins were tightly wrapped around their waists. This made it really risky in an accident.

Charioteers were slaves. If they won a race they would get a laurel wreath and some money. They might make enough to buy their freedom but most died young.

One celebrity driver called SCORPUS won over 2,000 races before being killed in a collision aged only 27.

Sea battles and bears

As time went on, the sports and spectacles that were staged in the Roman arenas became more and more bloodthirsty.

Sea battles

In the Colosseum the arena was specially constructed so that it could be flooded. Real sea battles were acted out. The ships rammed and fought each other. As they capsized the slave rowers drowned.

Wild animals

The Emperor would show off his wealth and power by capturing huge numbers of exotic wild animals from all corners of the Roman Empire.

These drawings are based on mosaics.

Lions, ostriches, bears, elephants, tigers, deer, rhinoceroses, leopards and panthers were slaughtered. During the celebration of the opening of the Colosseum 5,000 wild animals were killed in one day alone.

Sometimes the animals would hunt and kill each other. Unarmed slaves, criminals and Christians would also be savaged and killed by the beasts.